LAND OF THE FOUR DIRECTIONS

LAND OF THE

FOUR DIRECTIONS

Text and Photographs by
FREDERICK JOHN PRATSON

Introductions by
JOHN STEVENS and **ANDREW NICHOLAS, JR.**

THE CHATHAM PRESS, INC.
Old Greenwich, Connecticut

DISTRIBUTED BY THE VIKING PRESS, INC., NEW YORK

TO:
The children of the first People.

ACKNOWLEDGMENTS

I would like to express my gratitude to the following people whose friendship, help, and inspiration has made this book possible: Governor John Stevens; Governor Eugene Francis; Mr. Andrew Nicholas, Jr.; Chief Dennis Nicholas; Chief Albert Levi; Chief Peter Barlow; Mr. George Francis; Mr. Sam Augustine; The Albert Dana Family; The Tribal Councils of Indian Township and Pleasant Point; Edward and Priscilla Hinckley; Paul and Gretchen Coolidge; William "Cap'n Bill" Vinal; Mrs. Elsie Paul; The Union of New Brunswick Indians; Mr. Norman Bourque; Mr. John Hinshaw, my publisher; Mr. Christopher Harris, the book's designer; and most of all my wife, Patricia, for her vision and understanding.

FIRST EDITION

Copyright © 1970 by Frederick John Pratson

SBN 85699-016-7
Library of Congress Catalog Card Number 75-122759

Manufactured in the United States of America by
The Eastern Press, Inc., New Haven, Connecticut

CONTENTS

PREFACE

Throughout the United States and Canada, North American Indians are expressing the plight of their people with a new militancy. They are demanding that those in positions of power listen to what they have to say about the poverty and oppression they have lived with for so long and which they will tolerate no longer. Their words are not mere emotional threats; they are true statements of a harsh reality supported by a plethora of government, foundation, and private studies of the condition of contemporary Indians. When the North American Indian speaks, he does so with a genuine desire to improve the quality of life for his own people, as well as that of non-Indians, not to destroy what is good in our society.

Mr. Vine Deloria, a U.S. Sioux who wrote *Custer Died For Your Sins;* Mr. Harold Cardinal, a Canadian Cree and author of *The Unjust Society;* and N. Scott Momaday, a U.S. Kiowa and Pulitzer Prize winning author of the *House Made Of Dawn,* are Indian writers who have much to say to all humanity about how it is to be an Indian in today's world.

I am proud that two outstanding Indian leaders, John Stevens, Governor of the Passamaquoddy and Andrew Nicholas, Jr., Executive Director of the Union of New Brunswick Indians, have thought enough of this book to express their beliefs in its Introduction. They and other Indian leaders like them deserve the attention and support of the non-Indian for the sake of racial peace, justice, and progress.

The native people portrayed in this book are the Passamaquoddies of Indian Township and Pleasant Point, Maine; the Maliseet of Tobique Reserve; and the

Micmac of Big Cove and Indian Island, New Brunswick, Canada. They call themselves the first People by virtue of the fact that their ancestors were the first men and women to settle North America. In this book I refer to them as the "People," a loose translation of their own term and one they prefer to "Indian." These People and something of their way of life are shown here through photographs and text based on my own experiences, research, conversations, and insights. It has been my goal to portray both their problems and the richness of their human spirit. I recognize that my efforts are but brief glimpses, fragments, and images of a people who have so much more to say about themselves.

The Passamaquoddies, Maliseets, and Micmacs have been most generous to me. I consider many of them my friends for life, and I hope this portrait will please them.

—FREDERICK JOHN PRATSON
North Scituate, Massachusetts
March, 1970

INTRODUCTIONS

I

White men say the Indian has a problem; they call it the "Indian Problem." I believe the Indian's biggest problem is the white man. For too long the United States and Canadian governments have treated the Indian as children. They have insisted that to grow up the Indian must become a white man, live as a white man, think as a white man.

The fact is that we are not white; we are Indian. The roots of our heritage on this continent are far deeper than those of any other group, and our cultural traditions have been passed from generation to generation since unrecorded time. We are a race of men and women who are just as intelligent and capable as any other race; we are human beings who offer warmth and friendship to all peoples. When the white man stops insisting that the Indian adhere to his ways and allows us to live as Indians, the "Indian Problem" will be solved.

From here the Indian tribal leaders and councils could then solve for themselves the real problems: those of poverty, lack of education and job opportunities. We need white man's help in the form of financial and personal assistance, but we also need his respect for the ability of our leaders to fully govern their people. "Self-determination" has been a guideline in United States aid to underdeveloped nations. Why cannot the government apply these same principles to aid granted the Indian tribes?

President Nixon has shown little sympathy toward any minority group, much less the Indians. He is more concerned with honoring our commitments overseas than honoring commitments to his citizens at home. To the American Indian these commitments are legally binding treaties, solemnly made between honorable men of both races; yet they have been constantly broken by greedy, ignorant people. Another prominent man, Senator Edmund Muskie of my own state of Maine, could do much more toward helping my people than he has so far. While he has assisted us on several occasions of minor importance, it can hardly be said that he is a champion of the Indian.

Land of the Four Directions is the first book which truly presents the way of life, the real problems, and the hopes for the future of the Indians in eastern Maine and the Canadian Maritimes. It is fully endorsed by the joint tribal councils of the Passamaquoddies. I sincerely hope that it will be closely read and studied by many white leaders including Mr. Nixon and Mr. Muskie, as well as by people of all races who seek a better understanding of each other's problems.

In closing I wish to say that the Indian can teach the non-Indian at least one thing of importance about how to live. To the non-Indian, time is of more value than life. For Indians, time is secondary; life is sacred. The American Indian waits . . . but his patience grows thin.

—JOHN STEVENS
Governor of the Passamaquoddy

II

It is with a deep and sincere sense of pride that I write these prefacing remarks to *Land of the Four Directions* by Fred Pratson, a person who I, and many other Indians, will consider a friend the rest of our lives. His excellent book is an honest insight into Indian people and Indian communities which very few non-Indians really see or, perhaps, even care to see. It is a current portrayal of a proud people whose status is constantly being threatened by governments, indeed by non-Indian society itself, and is a tribute which I as an Indian would like to be able to articulate. In a sense this book is a message from the Indian people themselves which says:

> *"Look at me . . . I am an Indian, and I am damn well proud of it.*
> *People, movies and history books have tried to shame and humiliate me, but they have not succeeded.*
> *I've been the brunt of many injustices. I, along with my blood-brothers and sisters, am a living example of man's inhumanity to man.*
> *Most levels of government have seen the pathetic conditions, the misery and the Indian's desire to play a meaningful role toward rectifying these situations, but they have not listened, they have not really heard. In most instances they have simply rolled over and played dead."*

In Canada today, just as it was one hundred years ago, there are established commandments of nameless, faceless mandarins in the federal government who dictate the fate of Indian people. From positions of complete isolation far removed from reality these high salaried, political appointees design government policies which govern the lives of a people they have never seen. They relish the thought that they, and they alone, know what is good for the Indian and have all the answers to the Indian's problems.

The truth is that they have no respect for the Indian people. Prime Minister Pierre Trudeau, generally known as the "swinging" leader of the Canadian government, has made some frightening public statements, and it is evident that he is completely uninformed about the status of the Indian. The policy statement of June, 1969, made by Trudeau's Minister of Indian Affairs, Jean Chretien, reflects his distorted concept of the situation. Basically, this statement is similar to the "termination policy" of the United States government made in the late 1950's. The disastrous results of this policy to the Indians of the United States should make the Canadian government realize this is not the answer, but as I have said, this administration is so lost in a world of unreality that it will not listen.

Here in New Brunswick 4,300 Micmacs and Maliseets live today in much the same way as they did many thousands of years ago. Theoretically the land is still theirs, but obligations to them made by their forebears in honorable treaties have been disregarded. The proposals made by Trudeau, if accepted by the Indians, will only serve to further jeopardize our negotiating position. Instead, the hopes of the Indian people lie to a large extent in the understanding and sympathy of the general public.

This book projects a plea from the Indian to look at us and at our conditions. If he does, the non-Indian will find no threats or schemes against anyone; he will see only a sincere desire to live in a world of peace, friendship, and mutual respect with people of all races.

—ANDREW NICHOLAS, JR.
Executive Director,
Union of New Brunswick Indians

We saw the eagle and our spirits soared with it into the sun.

THE LAND:
MORE THAN PROPERTY

Who was first in North America: a Viking warrior, an Italian sailing under the flag of Spain, a Puritan by way of Leyden and Plymouth?

The Indians are said to have reached the Land of the Four Directions some ten to thirty millenniums ago, thousands of years before the birth of Christ. The Puritans came just over three hundred years ago, Columbus slightly under five hundred, the Vikings perhaps a thousand.

When Europeans first discovered this continent, they described its people as being very friendly, helpful, and enchanting. Many explorers and settlers attributed their survival in a hostile environment to the help provided by the inhabitants who already knew its ways. Europeans called them Indians, a name derived as a result of a navigational error and one which they have borne ever since.

These people called themselves by many names long before the Europeans came: Passamaquoddy, Micmac, Maliseet, Mohawk, Crow, Blackfoot, and many more.

To them each name represents a distinct group of people, a separate political state; to call a Passamaquoddy a Mohawk is an insult as grievous as to call a Frenchman a German.

Without their land, the People would cease to live and be. Their land is more than a place on which to live and raise a family; it is an intimate part of their way of life. The land belongs to the community, although each family may use a portion on which to build a home. The land helps to maintain the community as a cohesive unit. It is the tabernacle of their race and culture, the repository of their dead and their history, and the supplier of their physical and spiritual nourishment.

The land is their past, present, and future.

Almost every conflict the People have had with non-Indians has been over land; yet they have always regarded themselves as only custodians of an earth belonging to Manitou, spiritual ruler of the Universe.

The non-Indian has yet to accept the fact that the land and its inhabitants are inseparable. To deprive the People of their land is to destroy them.

The sight of the circling gulls,
the sudden appearance of the beaver from his lodge,
the silver flash of salmon in the Miramichi,
the muted sound of the forest, and the peace of
the rivers created an indissoluble union between
the people and their wilderness world.

While life for the People has long been difficult, often cruel, there has existed for them a harmony between man and nature—a harmony that has made their life meaningful and many times joyous.

Hunting and fishing are big business; state and provincial laws maintain these sports for those who are able to pay.

Yet these same laws have been used at times to deny the People full accessibility to those lands where hunting and fishing are vital to their way of life—a deep physical and spiritual necessity.

It is a land of trees, mostly pine for paper pulp. The truck loaded high with cut sections of pine is a familiar sight as it roars down the highway passing with a wind and pressure that rocks the heavy car. Many of the People work in the forest or at the mill. It is one of the few places where a man can get a job. But the People are now increasingly looking to a future for their children beyond the work in the forest or at the mill.

28

THE COMMUNITY

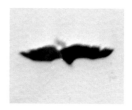

Almost every community is located near a body of water: a lake, a river, or the sea. The church with its high steeple is the focal point. A school, a community hall, a general store, a rectory for the priest, a home for the teaching nuns, and the homes of the People are arranged according to a formal street plan. Some of the communities support a craft shop for visiting tourists. One community has a modest stadium where traditional festivals are held. The village is open, except for a few old trees which provide spots of shade. There is usually a forest nearby where the People can obtain firewood, wild game, berries, roots, herbs, and traditional solitude. By and large the communities are remote and insular.

The People are not proud of the litter in some of their yards, nor are they satisfied with shack-like homes made from cast away materials. In one community rats which have bitten children and constantly carry the threat of disease are a serious problem. These are real conditions of poverty which the People are trying to solve with what money and education is available to them.

Many visitors come and leave, seeing only the squalor. Yet if they observed more closely they would see an ordered community where homes and yards range from neat and clean to worn and partially cared for to dangerous shelters and littered grounds. They would see new construction of houses, schools, roads, water and waste treatment plants. In short, they would discover their own town's appearance, only many gradations less affluent. The communities of the People are the poorest of the rural poor, but their efforts to improve and develop what is their own, with little help from outside the reserve, are never-ending.

The nearby non-Indian town can be a hostile place of suspicion, intolerance, ridicule, and injustice directed at the People. If the town could be avoided or ignored, its prejudices would not matter; but, the children have to go to school there, and the People need many of the goods and services sold by the town's stores.

Confrontations between non-Indians and the People are inevitable. They are last to be served or totally ignored at a store or restaurant; refused a haircut; given insults or angry looks. Policemen watch for the slightest cause for arrest or humiliation.

The non-Indian town is a place of a different race with a different religion and different ways. Both worlds coexist but not without a sense of deep tension and bitterness.

It was Fire Prevention Week and the teaching nuns passed out Junior Fire Marshal hats to their small students; circulars describing fire prevention ideas for the home were given to parents. Outside, sitting on blocks without hose or fresh paint, loomed the remains of the community's fire engine. To the children, it was a piece of play equipment.

The nearest operating fire department was in the town of non-Indians, some fifteen minutes away. When there was a fire in a home on the reserve, the structure usually burned to the ground before help arrived. Every response by the fire department was followed by a bill of over one hundred and fifty dollars to be paid from meager tribal funds.

The children wore their Junior Fire Marshal hats all week and played on the skeleton of their fire engine.

THE INDIVIDUAL

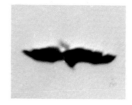

"*E*verybody in the world is going through some process. They say the Indian
must go through the process so that he can make it in the world.
We don't want to be processed Indians.
We don't want to be processed anything.
We just want to be ourselves."

As long as a man is a member of his tribe, he need never feel alone. He is known by everyone in his community. He can listen to stories about his forefathers and walk on the same land they walked on for as long as man can remember. He can go away to the city for work or to a foreign land in the military service of his country and know that he can always return and be welcomed. He knows there is a place where someone will always call him son, brother, friend.

The acts of an individual are subordinate to the interest and welfare of the People. Tribal leaders and spokesmen may make commitments which seem definite to the outsider but which are subject to being approved or overruled by a consensus vote of the tribal council and the People. An individual who is neither chief nor council member has the power to argue against a position taken by the entire community and win, if his convictions are firm and his reasoning sound.

The People honor a man primarily for what he has done for his community, not for what he has done for himself.

Each adult faces the fundamental problem of either staying in the community or leaving. If he stays, he knows that his choices for personal success (in non-Indian terms) are almost non-existent. If he can achieve a modestly comfortable living for himself and his family, he will consider himself fortunate. The main advantage to staying is that he can remain close to the people and traditional ways he has known all his life. If he leaves the community to work and live in a large city, his economic and material opportunities increase, but the price is a certain alienation from his tribe. Some adjust to city life to the point where they make an almost complete break from their past. Others become so disheartened by an often oppressive, impersonal urban environment that they return to their former communities for good. A few have the ability and good fortune to balance life in the city with retreats to the communities for spiritual and psychological rejuvenation.

"*I* *went to Boston to sell some Christmas trees.*
Everybody called me 'Big Chief.'
They thought it would make me feel good.
Everywhere I turned there were cars, buses, trucks,
and streetlights. I couldn't walk anywhere without worrying
about getting hit by one of them . . . or waiting
for a light to tell me when to stop and when to go.
Here, I can walk anywhere I want.
Nothing and no one will stop me.
Here, I am free."

Many of the women are beautiful; some of their faces reflect unmixed blood, and others reveal their Anglo-Saxon or French ancestry.

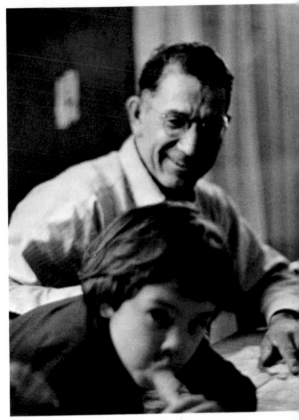

ENTER MY HOME

Once you are known and accepted, their homes are open to you and there is a feeling of genuine welcome.

A cup of coffee or tea is offered.

Sometimes you can spear a hunk of meat cooking in a large, black frying pan. If it is venison, it is savory and tastes better than the best beef. On the table are salt covered crackers and Indian flat bread.

You sit around a table of men, children, and women hacking away at a large cube of fresh farmer's butter. You spread it thick—something you would never do in the city—but here it's irresistible and absolutely delicious.

Hot Indian pot pie of dumplings, steak and spices, candied woodland berries, and home-made doughnuts covered with maple sugar frosting was the dinner the wife made. The invitation was an unexpected surprise after a long day of dismal winter weather and the necessity of relating to a constant stream of new faces. The warmth of the home and the family snuffed the growing weariness and depression in a stranger far from his own home. The food was eaten with great pleasure; a new zest returned to greet other members of the community even though the sun had long since gone down.

To feed and make strangers comfortable has always been one of the traditional ways of the People.

The kitchen is the center of life in the house. It is for eating, talking, planning, socializing, working, and sometimes for sleeping.

Some kitchens double as the T.V. room and the parlor; some are decorated with everything from national flags to religious pictures to souvenirs of Cape Cod or Cape Breton Island. Others are spartan, business-like, and empty of everything that is not an absolute necessity.

Some kitchens appear to be ideal breeding grounds for tuberculosis; others are scrubbed clean daily.

Each one gives a strong impression of the inhabitants within.

The house smells of cleaners and the walls shine with new enamel. The young, attractive housewife scrubs the floor on her knees, casting a threatening eye on those who would dare to enter with muddy feet. The supper is cooking, soon to be devoured by hungry school children and parents. The preschoolers play a wild game with their friends and dogs in the front yard while the older ones wrestle with algebra problems and sentence diagrams. The husband, a Ford Foundation Fellow, works at his plans for helping his people.

Into the dimness the ever present television set beams a strange world where affluence, comfort, purpose, and beauty are the norm and poverty is a documentary special.

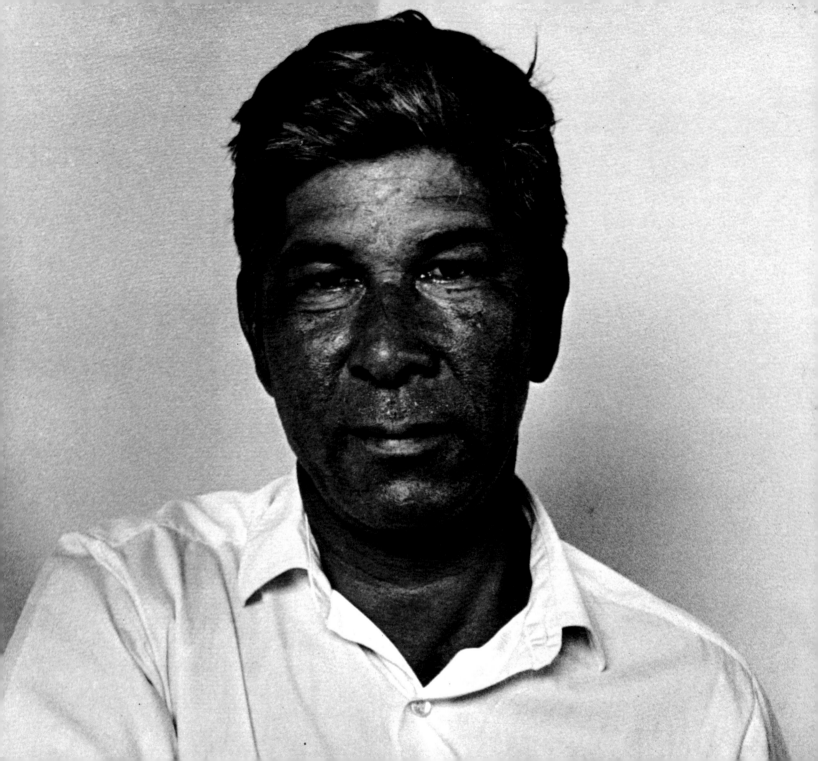

ROOTS OF A PEOPLE

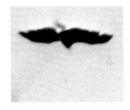

"I am not a Canadian or an American.
First, I am a Micmac.
Then, I am a North American.
Then, I am a Canadian or an American."

December 24, 1776

BROTHERS OF PASSAMAQUODIA:

I am glad to hear that you accepted the Chain of Friendship which I sent you last February from Cambridge, and that you are determined to keep it bright and unbroken.

Brothers, I have a piece of news to tell you which I hope you will attend to. Our enemy, the King of Great Britain, endeavored to stir up all the Indians from Canada to South Carolina against us. But our brethren of the six Nations and their allies the Shawnees and the Delawares would not hearken to the advice of his Messengers sent among them, but kept fast hold of the ancient covenant chain. The Cherokees and the Southern tribes were foolish enough to listen to them and take up the hatchet against us. Upon this our Warriors went into their country, burnt their houses, destroyed their corn and obliged them to sue for peace and give hostages for their future good behavior.

Now Brothers never let the king's wicked counsellor turn your hearts against me and your brethren of this country, but bear in mind what I told you last February and what I tell you now. In token of my friendship I send you this from my army on the banks of the Great River Delaware, this 24th day of December, 1776.

GEORGE WASHINGTON

Members of the Passamaquoddy tribe photographed in 1905 by Charles E. Brown of Perry, Maine.

The primary language of the People is a branch of the Algonquin tongue: Maliseet, Micmac, or Passamaquoddy. The children learn to speak their people's ancient language before English or French; school can be a difficult experience for both student and teacher. Such an inability to communicate frequently results in mutual frustration and very little teaching and learning are accomplished. Throughout his life, non-Indian society will discourage his use of the native tongue as being irrelevant and confusing and will demand that he use only French or English in his encounters with non-Indians. He is made to feel ashamed of his native tongue and learns that the non-Indian's language is essential for survival in an economic and social milieu controlled by non-Indians. In turn, non-Indian society makes almost no attempt to learn and understand anything of his language or ways.

"They make me feel like the foreigner who has just come here on the boat... to a land that has belonged to us for thousands of years."

A large poster of Geronimo, kneeling on one knee and gripping a rifle, is in the homes and offices of the more militant. His eyes penetrate the soul.

"What do you see in them?"
"Pain . . . that they have killed his people and taken his land . . . that they will not let him live in peace . . . that there is no other way but to fight and to kill . . . that he will not live to see his victory in the generation who looks to him now."

"*My life has been one of two different worlds; that of my people and that of the white man. This often forces me to be two different people when my desire is to be one whole person. I want to accept what is the best of both worlds and not be forced to deny one part of me in order to please those who want me to be only like them.*"

"*They have assumed the names and gestures of their enemies, but have held on to their own, secret souls; and in this there is a resistance and an overcoming, a long outwaiting.*"

—N. Scott Momaday
from *House Made of Dawn*

The slogans are a necessary response in an age which demands catchy one-liners:

INDIAN POWER!
REMEMBER WOUNDED KNEE MASSACRE!
CUSTER DIED FOR YOUR SINS!

The time for being docile and accepting is ending. Commitment is contagious and growing.

There is a yearning to rediscover the old ways; they have tired of trying to live like the non-Indian. For many, the sacrifice for this compromise has been the loss of their traditional customs, language, and history. When one is faced with unemployment, illness, and apathy, it is difficult to promote culture.

This has been a loss not only to the People but to all North Americans. Most important, it has been a loss of centuries of the creative energies of a most talented and intelligent people.

Movements to create cultural awareness and productivity are spreading through the communities; old ways are again being taken seriously, especially by the young.

Perhaps the young people will bring about a renaissance of a culture that has been asleep too long.

Despite many difficulties, the old ways manage to persist in the language, food, crafts, and dances of the People. On special occasions some dress in fringed leather garments decorated with multicolored, intricate symbols and wear eagle or hawk feathers in their hair.

Several of their festivals, such as the choosing of a princess or a feast in honor of fiddleheads (ferns cut at springtime and used as a vegetable), are open to the general public. But the ways of the People are private to them, and it is the rare outsider who is privileged to experience even a hint of what has tenuously survived for centuries.

The history books the children study often portray their ancestors as savages, killers, or retarders of Western civilization. Seldom is mention made of how their ancestors helped the non-Indian survive on this continent, or how their forefathers were deprived of their culture and land, or of the hunger, disease, and hate they were forced to endure.

A portrait of Queen Elizabeth and Prince Philip, the Maple Leaf flag of Canada and the Provincial colors hang on the wall of every classroom in New Brunswick. Symbols of the People's own heritage are rare; it is a unique teacher who attempts to convey the old culture and traditions to the child.

In Maine many Passamaquoddy homes bear another portrait on their walls: that of John F. Kennedy. Hung with honor near a small American flag, a piece of holy palm, a statue of a saint, the Virgin or Christ, the portrait is a reminder of a president who truly wanted to understand and help; a symbol of what might have been and a hope that life may yet improve.

When they dance, the young show the energy of warriors. Their movements are lightning rapid; each is a new surprise executed with virile force and determination. The elders applaud, admire, and wish that the young could forge their destinies with the same lack of inhibitions.

But they also see themselves in a boy dancer and feel the layers of broken promises, shattered hopes, and privations that have accumulated within them since their youth. They wonder if life will be better for the boy who dances like a warrior.

At a traditional dance, some of the People feel self-conscious, and the dance leaders must pull them to their feet and keep them moving. But the beating of the drum, the shaking of the rattles, and the chanting of the tenor have their effect; soon snaking lines and whirling circles are formed, binding the People in the joy and ritual of their ancestors.

Even those who choose to remain standing along the periphery are touched by the music and the dancing; its message reminds them never to forget the old ways.

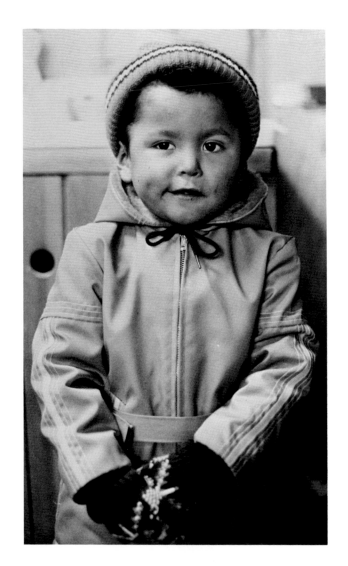

A good sense of humor is much prized by the People, especially when it is
directed at oneself.

"We want to know Christianity through our ancient ways, not just through the ways of the non-Indian. We want to believe that what we know within us is true. To be forced to believe otherwise is to destroy what we are."

Passamaquoddy Lord's Prayer

N'miktausen Spemkik èhime Sagmanwelmegudets èliwizyinj Ketepeitem-
waghen petzussewitchj Keteleltemwaghenuli tsiksetagudets yuttel Ktah-
kemigook, tahalo te Spemkik. Miline tekètch bemghiskak etaskiswè nta-
panemen, te anehètemohuyeku ntwabellokewaghe nenuool tahalo nlon eli
aneheltemohuyekù ewabellokedjik; te ekkwi losseline unemiotwaghenek
wedji ghighihine tannik medzikkil.

Nialètch

More and more of the People turn away from the established Christian faith toward movements which seek to bring back the ancient beliefs. The addition of tom-toms to the ritual of the Mass is not enough to turn apathy into excitement. They view the priest or minister who is afraid to leave the solitude of his big house as a millstone around their necks instead of an example of virtue and piety. Many are tired of waiting for the "blackrobe" who would convey a sense of joy and hope by walking freely among the People, seeking their opinions, and trying to solve their real-life problems.

The faces of the nuns are old, young, long, lean, chubby, wrinkled, pretty. Some reveal repressed frustration; others give a sense of sanctity. Everyday they contribute to the People by teaching their children. Some reflect their ignorance of the People's ways and judge them according to their own values. Some say very little but work quietly, winning the respect and love of most of the villagers.

Their life is that of a community within a community. One nun felt that she could never leave the People; she lies buried among them on a hilltop graveyard, looking toward Passamaquoddy Bay.

The anthropologists come into the communities asking the tribal councils for permission to study the People in order to earn an advanced degree or write a book. They are sincere scholars in their quest to further knowledge. The People are generous in the giving of their time and their memories. Sometimes the attention is flattering and can kill the boredom for a few hours, but often they feel like living curiosities in a woodland extension of a university museum.

Many bright, well meaning non-Indians come to them with ideas they say will solve all the People's problems. They go away puzzled when their ideas are rejected.

Somewhere in their plans they have failed to realize the fundamental need of the People to remain culturally themselves.

A MAN WOULD RATHER WORK

The People are often regarded as lazy or unreliable employees. They are no better or worse than any other racial group; it is their philosophy toward work which is different from that of most other people. They do not react against work itself but to the way it is presented and what they consider the impersonality of the industrial system. They can be productive, reliable, and loyal when the system makes some concessions to their life style. An individual responsible for producing a set quantity of a product over a flexible time span will take greater pride in his achievements than one who sells his time on an eight-hour, five-day-a-week basis.

The People need the benefits of an industrial society, but want to be masters over methods and machines, not slaves of technology.

The communities are remote from urban, manufacturing, financial, and transportation centers. Finding a nearby job is extremely difficult when local businesses are not expanding and large industrial concerns are not attracted to locations so distant from their markets.

Vocational training programs turn out people with skills that often must be sold far from one's home.

The realists among the People are not waiting for some manufacturer to settle on their land and provide lease money for tribal coffers or jobs for the people. They know this will probably never happen. Instead, many are seeking a more direct control over their economic destinies through such devices as the cooperative movement. These movements provide programs designed to teach people how to create and manage their own industries and stores. Divergent human interests and dedication make such communal projects difficult and complex, but it is in the psychology and traditions of the People to work and think as a group.

The Passamaquoddies of Maine are eligible to receive free, government surplus food. The program is recent; before it went into operation the People often went hungry and suffered from malnutrition and other diseases associated with poor diet.

A representative of each family comes to a central place in the community, such as the basement of a school. Here he receives canned meat, dried eggs, flour, crackers, dried fruit, coffee, and other foods which are recorded in a ledger bearing his name.

The People feel that they would rather work to feed their families, but when that is impossible the free food is the only alternative.

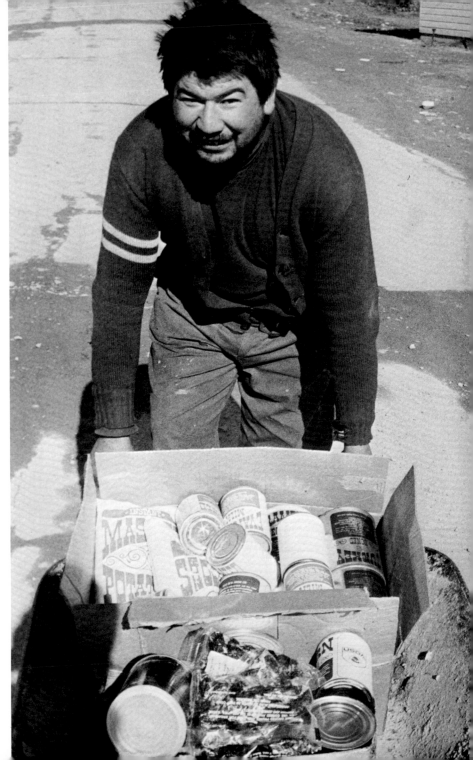

The young men are studying to become carpenters under a manpower training program provided by the Canadian government. The non-Indian teacher compliments his students, saying that they are intelligent, determined, and potentially very skillful. The courses in blueprint reading, mathematics, specifications, estimating, and such are conducted in the community hall on the reserve. On-the-job training is provided by allowing the men to work on the new housing the Canadian government is building for the People on the reserve. The program relates the new vocational training to marketable skills in demand both on and off the reserve.

The future carpenters take a break from their studies and form teams on either side of the hall to play a wild game of Micmac style tennis. Part of the team stands against the wall on a level about a foot higher than the line in front. They roll newspapers and magazines into rackets and establish an imaginary net between them. The ball is served by one side and slammed back by the other. The play, which continued for almost an hour, involves about fourteen excited, shouting, laughing, fast moving young men.

The People are fine artists and craftsmen, but because of economic necessity, many turn art as a means of self-expression into a paying commodity for the tourist trade.

A walk through their homes brings many surprises: complex ash and sweet grass baskets of beautiful and tasteful designs made by Passamaquoddy women; traditional war clubs with heads of animals, birds, reptiles, and abstract symbols sculpted by Maliseet carvers; silk screen graphics and paintings of legends by Micmac artists; woven patterns in textiles; and ax handles shaped with precision from ash logs. Every piece is made by hand with talent and pride.

These artists face the dilemma of creative people everywhere; how to create from the soul and feed the body?

CHILDREN

The young see the community as a large family. This is a world in which a child is warmly accepted in almost every home. His fellow students in the early grades are friends and relatives. The child is able to play in the streets and yards long after sunset and eats his meals when he is hungry, not when a bell rings or a clock strikes. For awhile in their lives, they are indulged by adults and the children feel and give happiness.

For these same young, it can also be a time of crippling illnesses treated too late or of an early death from pneumonia. Life can be gnawing pangs of hunger when food has run out or the sight of a mother and father drunk.

The pain inflicted by a bigot when the child is in his town results in confusion and hurt and an end to childhood innocence about the non-Indian world.

The school on the reservation is within sight of a child's home. Whatever the problems in school, friends and relatives and home are waiting just outside the door.

But the day comes when the child must get on the yellow bus and travel to the non-Indian school. Though the ride can be measured in minutes, it is felt to be as distant as Mars is from earth. From the moment the child enters this new school until the day he leaves, he is made to feel different, and these differences are not experienced with pride or confidence. Almost no effort is made to understand his ways and, in turn, he finds less and less reason to learn the ways of the non-Indian.

The psychological and spiritual hurt, the boredom, the loneliness, and the alienation are partly relieved when he decides never again to ride that yellow bus.

"*How* would you like it if everywhere you went someone called you 'injun,' 'redskin,' 'Big Chief,' or worse?

How do you think it feels when you are asked how it is to live in a tepee and why you are not wearing a war bonnet?

They say to each other, 'Watch out for him or he'll scalp you.'

Our girls are never just girls . . . they're always squaws.

Everything about us is a big joke to them. It's hard for them to understand why an Indian must be proud of being what he is."

97

The children make ink blot designs on paper and write sentences describing what the images mean to them. Most of the black shapes are abstract and surrealistic, but young eyes quickly discover familiar animals, persons, or events. Out of clay they make complete model villages of their people the way they looked decades ago. Their art is colorful, exciting, joyous; each child is proud to display his work. Many of the classrooms have closed circuit television and sophisticated learning aides. But the classes that generate a momentum of lively learning are only those led by rare vital and creative teachers, rich in their understanding of these unique pupils.

It is eleven thirty in the morning; the children put away their books. They are led down the stairs to the school basement. They are excited; there is much confusion and noise as they take their seats around long tables. Women serve steaming bowls of thick fish chowder, salt crackers, bread, milk, and canned fruit cocktail to the children for their government sponsored school lunch.

Late that afternoon, a boy asks the adult visitor when he will eat supper that evening. The answer is given and the boy is asked when he will eat his. The boy says there will be no supper for him. The adult asks him about breakfast the next morning. The boy replies that there will be no breakfast. The boy says he will have to wait until the next school lunch.

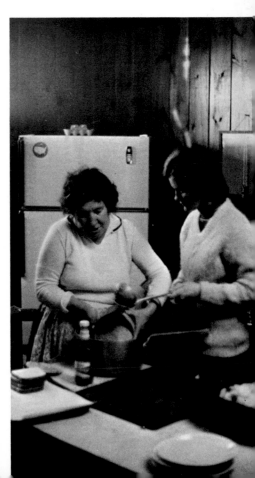

Skeleton frames of swings, monkey bars, revolving platforms, and slides, gray metallic in color and worn with frequent use, are behind or to the side of the elementary schools. Each recess the children climb, push, swing, rush, ride these creations of an uninspired toy maker. But it is the stacked rows of concrete sewer pipes, rough wooden planks across a fresh dirt pile, wire mesh and other materials destined for dull utilitarian projects that are first put to use by the children as innovative gymnasiums; playgrounds of endless imaginary happenings.

They call the ten year old retarded boy "Man" or "Fellow." He crawls instead of walks and makes sounds instead of talks. While the family is poor, they give "Man" love and a hope that someday he will improve. The local doctor told the parents the boy would outgrow his sickness; the state hospital has him on a list that someday may say it's his turn now. In the meantime, "Man" sets out plastic railroad tracks in a rectangle around the room and laughs and cries in his own private world.

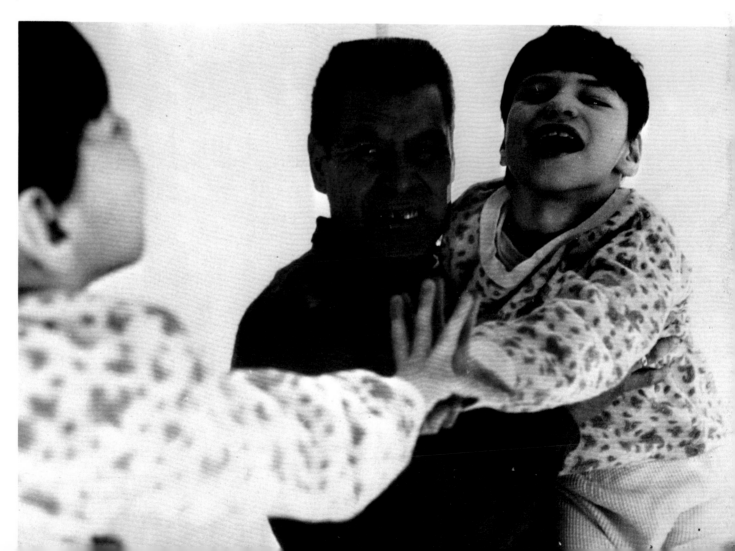

The little girls are shy at first. With some coaxing, they come out from behind the pickup truck and surround you, asking questions, poking their fingers into the camera's lens, and incessantly pulling at the back of your coat as you frame the perfect pose and press the shutter release.

Surprise!

Much laughter.

104

Their joy is more valuable than a thousand perfect pictures.

She holds a dead sparrow in fingers that caress the soft, still form.
She thrusts it forward proudly.
It is her pet and her toy.
No remorse that it is a dead bird; only a contentment that she can at last grasp
something so often beyond reach.

There are about fifteen boys on each side. Crouched in position, they growl fiercely at each other. The ball is snapped back to the quarterback and both lines collide. The quarterback tries an end run but is cut off by determined tacklers. He spots a receiver in the distance and heaves a pass toward him; the boy catches it and runs down the field toward the goal. He is overtaken and pulled down. They pile on top of him, first the other side, then his own teammates. Everyone is in or on top of a pile of legs, arms, heads, rear ends. The boy with the ball must be squashed, crushed beyond recognition.

After the pile sways back and forth a few times, they peel off. The boy at the bottom still grips the ball. They all laugh at each other and quickly form two lines and start all over again.

They slam their fists into each other's bodies and faces. One has the look of a winner and the other is close to defeat. Their movements are quick; the punches sharp. The wounded one is forced to his knees, trying to defend himself from the onslaught while attempting to inflict pain on the other.

An older girl runs out to break it up before the victor is decided.

A woman's inclination is to prevent pain and conflict. But the world these young boys will soon face is hostile to them, and their fight is but a preparation for the more complex struggles ahead.

The boy plays a piper's tune on his whistle and the children gather around him. His face is smeared and a dead fingernail hangs soon to be plucked. Nothing disturbs his music. The children gather around him, listening and dreaming. They perch on a playground platform that revolves when pushed. It starts to move in a laborious circle, speeding ever faster into a whirl of children's images and the sound of the whistle.

It slowed and stopped. They got off and he put away the whistle. The schoolbell rang. They walked toward the waiting nun. A door slammed shut and everything became quiet.

The pregnant young woman sits in the sunlight filtering through the kitchen window.

What are her thoughts about this coming child?
Will its future be any better?

THOSE OF AGE

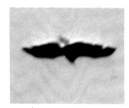

For the unemployed teenage boy who is also a high school dropout, the game is how to beat the boredom.

A few rounds on the pool table is a cure for awhile. Wait for the weekend dance; find a date; get drunk; think about going to the city for a job; think about joining the army or the marines; steal a car; get arrested and thrown into jail; smoke pot; knock up a girl; sit around; talk; sleep.

Still, the boredom is not beaten. Day after day, hardly anything changes.

The place is Memramcook Institute in a sleepy Acadian village of New Brunswick. Here teenagers representing Indian youth from Maine and the Canadian Maritimes meet to discuss ways to solve their high school dropout problem and improve the quality of their education. During the first days of the meeting they listen to speeches by many distinguished educators, resource people, and their own leaders. The adults dominate the gathering; the young seem passive and unparticipating.

Midpoint in the conference, a dramatic change takes place. The young people hold closed meetings among themselves, inviting only those adults who they feel can contribute to their discussions. When the conference ends, the young people have formulated a resolution:

"For too long we have watched our people who have attended public, government, and church schools. A few of the students have graduated; most have dropped away disillusioned, dispirited, and unable to make their way in the non-Indian world and often are of no value to their own people.

We intend this school to be different from existing schools.
We intend this school to be unique.
We will use new ideas, new methods, and new information.

We are determined to operate a program which will enable our people to hold their own with pride and dignity everywhere and to be valuable members of their own community."

Girls often become mothers before they are wed. The mother may become the butt of gossip, jokes, or snide remarks, but there is seldom a cruel, lasting condemnation.

She is the master of her own guilt or innocence. There is almost no stigma placed on her by the community; often the child is adopted by its grandmother and raised as one of her own.

Life is difficult enough for the People and they have long learned not to make it more so.

He is a general handy man who does odd jobs around the community like cutting evergreen boughs for the women to weave into Christmas wreaths; banking dirt around the foundations of houses for insulation from the sub-zero underdrafts of winter; or carting people's free food allotments home from the distribution point. He is of medium height with a growing beer belly, but from the way he handles both ax and shovel he probably has the strength of a black bear.

Most of the time he wears several days of hair on his face and a tattered pullover shirt. On seeing him for the first time, one feels threatened. But he always gives himself away by constantly smiling. It is difficult to remember a word that he spoke . . . but somehow he communicates.

116

On a Sunday afternoon you see the young men home on leave, trim and proud in their uniforms, with admiring children pulling at their sleeves and all about them. They are marines and soldiers; men who come from a long heritage of fierce fighters. You see them go into the homes of their mothers and sweethearts, perhaps for the last time.

A mother holds the stars and stripes folded into the triangle of a patriotic death; a symbol of the generosity of one who has given and who will continue to give.

To the non-Indians of the area he is only an Indian. They call him boy in the seacoast inn where they served us drinks.

This man who they call boy is the father of many children. He is a man who has overcome serious personal problems of a magnitude which would have defeated many a man—white, red, or black. He is a leader of his people, earnestly seeking new and better ways to improve their education, housing, health, and economic opportunities.

The non-Indians asked him to march in a holiday parade. He fought in Korea and still had his uniform. He put on his Marine Corps tunic, with the left side filled with battle ribbons and citations and sergeant's gold chevrons sewn against the indigo sleeve.

Non-Indians call him a charismatic leader of the Maine Passamaquoddies. As a political figure, he is not without his enemies and severe critics. He listens more than he talks, yet is equally able to communicate effectively with his own people, non-Indian politicians, scholars, the press, and the young. He travels widely, speaking at universities and attending meetings with other Indian leaders. When there is no other recourse, he dons traditional garments and leads protests against unresolved injustices. His goals are to unify his people into one voice; to direct their talents in the solution of their own problems; to develop a continuum of good leadership; and to make the best possible use of all available resources to improve their economic and cultural life.

He is also a former Marine, decorated for service in the Korean War, and a family man. A dropout who has earned a high school equivalency through home study, he was elected president of a nonprofit corporation to establish an international independent school to reclaim educational dropouts. He was elected to this position by representatives of the Passamaquoddy, Penobscot, Micmac, and Maliseet peoples from Maine, New Brunswick, Nova Scotia, and Prince Edward Island.

His wish is to see other capable people step forward and accomplish more than he has.

Another leader, from New Brunswick, Canada, finds his major challenges stemming from the prejudices and intolerance of the dominant non-Indian society; the Canadian federal government's termination and restrictive policies; and from his Maliseet and Micmac peoples whose differences sometimes make their progress very difficult.

The programs to which he devotes his energies involve upgrading the people's educational level; furthering the economic development of their communities; reclaiming dropouts; and strengthening the new union between the Maliseet and Micmac peoples so that they can solve each other's problems. His position requires the talents of a master politician, diplomat, engineer, economist, educator, administrator, mass media expert, and anthropologist. He travels throughout his province, his nation, and into the United States to present the views and needs of the Maliseets and Micmacs to the press, the general public, and to the political, academic, and commercial establishments.

A university graduate and a professional civil engineer, he is a young man who already has "made it" in the white man's world. He is a devoted family man and a gentleman but one who is firm in his resolve to see the People receive their rightful place in North American society.

He could have assimilated himself in the non-Indian's world, but his decision was to be what he really is and to help his people.

The teacher is one of the People. She is lovely, bright, and alert with the children. On the walls of her classroom are symbols of her people's way of life. And there is pride in herself and in the students when she shows their work.

Once they had no choice but to protest. They had asked the State government to help solve some of their medical problems, but the State answered with promises instead of action. The needs of the People could not wait; they were too familiar with the fate of governmental promises. Something had to be done to dramatize the situation so that public opinion would demand justice from the government.

A major U.S. highway runs through their township. They decided to block this highway with their bodies and charge a toll for every car, truck, and bus that came through. The young, the old, mothers with babies in their arms, children dressed in traditional garments, formed a human blockade on the highway. Each driver was stopped and asked to pay a toll to be used to buy the medical services the People required. A few dollars were collected before the State Police came and dragged the People away from the road. Some were jailed; others were hurt; but the People won their battle. The State government agreed to take action immediately.

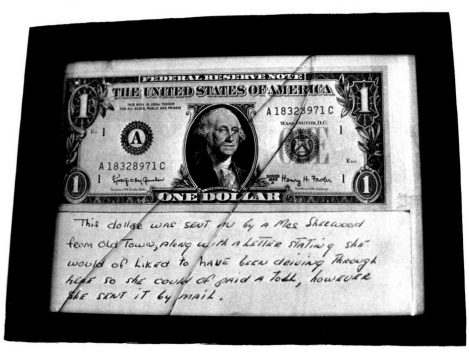

THE ELDERS

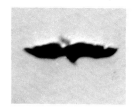

The old remember the past, tell their stories, and wait for death.

The old are not rejected; they continue to hold a place of importance in their families and in the community. Some elders serve as members of the tribal council and are very active in the affairs governing the lives of the People. Many work at odd jobs around the community or at their crafts making baskets and ax handles.

The illnesses of old age plague them, but they are stoic about the pain and discomfort. A cigarette, a shot of whiskey, a grandchild on the lap, or a good T.V. program make a day pass comfortably.

It is difficult to age gracefully under the circumstances that have affected their lives . . . but most manage, somehow.

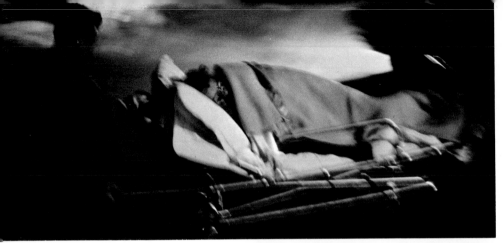

The night is cold, but children play outdoors in the dim light from the windows of kitchens and bedrooms. The harsh wail of a siren cuts the night; an ambulance turns into the street. It stops at an old woman's home, and medics rush in with a stretcher. A crowd gathers in front of her small home to watch as she is carried on the stretcher to the ambulance.

The ambulance leaves; the old woman is gone.

Death visited the community three times during that month. Two of the people were old and death was expected, but the other was a young man with a large family to support. The people weep deeply at his loss.

The graveyards in the communities appear neglected; weeds and litter obscure the delineations of individual plots. The wooden crosses are weather-worn and will probably never again have a coat of fresh paint; some lie at odd angles on the stony ground or tilt in a ditch.

The dead are not forgotten, but the hardships of survival preempt the attention of the living.

We talk about death. I ask him what his people think of the afterlife. He replies that everyone will be in some future happiness.

I ask him about justice. If someone wrongs the innocent in life, why should he be rewarded after death along with the good? He replies that those who do wrong are punished enough while they live.

EPILOGUE

It is not too late for the Indian and the non-Indian to work together toward improving the quality of their lives. The Indian has expressed his desire to be an equal partner with the non-Indian ever since their first contact, hundreds of years ago. While some individual non-Indians have responded with genuine friendship, history indicates that most non-Indians have been more interested in domination than in equal partnership. History is the reality of the past; its often pathetic record of the shoddy treatment of the Indian does not have to be the reality of the future.

Today, the Indian desperately needs more training, funds, technical advice, and most of all, the freedom to develop himself and his own resources in his own way. Both the United States and Canada preach and support the philosophy of self-determination of peoples around the world. It is now time that both nations permit this same human right to be exercised by their own native people.

In the past the Indian helped us to survive and prosper in what was a strange and hostile land. In today's world where the natural environment has become poisonous, congested, and ugly; where human society struggles more in the realm of the absurd than in a climate of reason, the Indian is again prepared to help the non-Indian survive. He can teach us how to live in harmony with nature, our family, our community, and ourselves. We have developed sophisticated technologies which provide an easier and more productive life, and lost much of our dignity in the process. Though the Indian looks to us for some of the answers to his problems, we should not overlook the fact that he may provide some solutions to our own.